Funded by

MISSION COLLEGE
Carl D. Perkins Vocational and Technical Education Act Grant

Christmas

Christmas flowers include bouquets, arrangements and all other possible decorations.
Flowers as well as botanical and artificial materials provide colour, texture and fragrance.
Flowers can be used to communicate emotions such as joy, hope, expectation
and the warmth of friendship, especially at Christmas.
The design is determined by the message they have to convey. The possibilities are
endless but the technique should always take the needs of the living material into account.

Per, Max and Tomas

Creativity with flowers

Christmas

Per Benjamin
Max van de Sluis
Tomas De Bruyne

stichting
kunstboek

Garlands

The history of Christmas flowers

Although the Three Wise Men did not bring baby Jesus any, flowers have featured in Christmas rites and rituals for many centuries. But long before the birth of Jesus, people in many parts of Europe and the rest of the world have been celebrating the winter solstice. People celebrate the end of winter and look forward to days getting longer and lighter. These celebrations are commonly seen as the precursor to the Christmas celebrations we know today. The use of Christmas trees and flowers dates back to the early 1600s in Germany and central Europe. But let's look at how Christmas traditions came about, how old pagan traditions merged with Christian ones, and, finally, how we see and use flowers and greenery today.

The history of Christmas dates back to 2000 BC. Many of our Christmas traditions existed centuries before the Christ child was born. Most ancient peoples of the world worshipped the sun, celebrating the winter solstice. They believed winter ended the sun god's rule, allowing the evil powers of darkness to take over and kill things. As the day grew shorter and the night longer, they feared the sun god would not return. Late December was a turning point, days grew longer and sunlight stronger. People held festivals to welcome the sun god's return.

The celebration of the winter solstice dates back to ancient times in Mesopotamia; houses were decorated with garlands and wreaths; greenery and flowers served as a reminder of summer. Especially green was important as it was and still is considered to bring luck. The Greeks and Romans celebrated their pagan gods. Especially during their winter festival of Saturnia, the Romans – decorated with garlands of laurel (Laurus) and evergreens – lighted candles, exchanged laurel wreaths, and gave green plants as gifts, mostly holly (Ilex) for good luck. Even the cutting of green trees and covering them in silver and gold are mentioned in texts. (Could it have been a predecessor of our Christmas tree and decorations?)

People in the rest of Europe held similar midwinter sun festivals. December feasts were common in Europe, also because it was necessary to slaughter cattle that could not be fed during the winter and so the meat would be preserved in cold weather. With the completion of the harvest and snow on the ground, farmers had more than enough provisions. As there was not much work to be done, they had ample time to relax, feast, celebrate and engage in social activities. Early Europeans believed in evil spirits, witches, ghosts and trolls. As the winter solstice approached with its long cold nights and short days, many people feared the sun would not return. Special ritual celebrations were held to lure back the sun. Bonfires were lit, evergreens, ivy (Hedera) and greenery were brought indoors to clear the air and brighten the mood during the long, dreary winter. Boughs or wreaths of holly – believed to have magical powers as they remained green throughout the harsh winter – were often placed over doors to keep evil spirits away. Apples, nuts, cones were tied to branches, as a reminder of summer.

At first, the Christian church forbade this kind of celebration, wanting to keep the birthday of Jesus a solemn and religious affair. But, eventually, it was decided that the pagan

'Table' Christmas tree

celebration would be toned down and turned into a celebration fit for the son of God. It was also decided to make the four-week period before Christmas a time of prayer and preparation for the ensuing holy festival, called Advent, which means 'coming'.

Flower creations were made more or less in the same way and similar techniques used from Roman times until the 17-18th century. Wreaths were woven on thick strings or plaits which served as the basis. Flowers and foliage were tied and sometimes sewed around the base. Garlands were made in the same way: the back was made from packed hay and grass, while the front-facing part was decorated. These could either hang freely or on walls and doors.

Mainly the church and the upper classes used flowers. During the Middle Ages, we see a great decline in the use of flowers because of church policy, but later they gave in and incorporated pagan traditions into Christian rituals.

In royal courts and amongst the rich, money was spent on staging parties at Christmas and dinners with magnificent table decorations, garlands and wreaths hanging from the ceilings, on walls and beside tables. It was also popular to use evergreens and, when available, petals on the floor for their scent to cover less delicate smells! Materials for

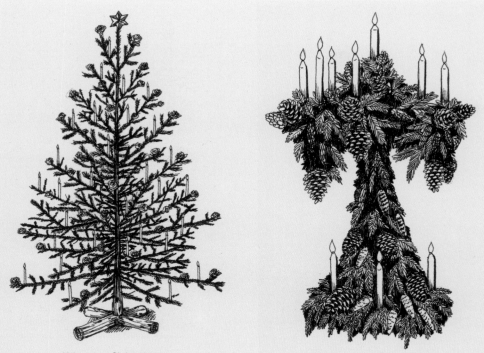

19th century Christmas tree   19th century candle arrangement

Christmas were sparse, so florists had to use evergreens, ivy, holly mixed with branches, berries, fruits, cones, nuts and even flowers made from paper.

The most popular colours were red and green, traditional Christmas colours. Green is the colour of nature, growth, the fields, hope and spring. At Christmas time – as was the case during ancient winter festivals – green represents our hope that spring will return and reign victorious over winter. Red is associated with the heart and emotions, especially feelings of love and suffering, and the Christian virtue of charity. Red is the colour of Christ who suffered for humankind. It is the colour of his courage and his sacrifice. Legend has it that holly sprang from the footsteps of Christ as he walked the earth. The pointed leaves represented the crown of thorns, and the red berries symbolised the blood he shed on the cross. But, we see that even the colours and materials are a mix of old pagan traditions and Christian customs.

The Christmas tree, as we know it, was first seen in the 16th century, and was not popular outside of Germany until the 19th century. At first, trees were only about two feet (66 cm) tall and placed on tables. Legend has it that the Protestant reformer Martin Luther first adorned trees with light. While coming home one December evening, the beauty of the stars shining through the branches of a fir inspired him to recreate the effect by placing candles on the branches of a small fir tree inside his home. Most decorations were pretty sweets, biscuits, fruits and other items meant to be admired and eaten by guests. These trees were sometimes called 'sugar trees'. Later paper ornaments became popular. Finally, in the late 1800s, glass ornaments and electric lights made their debut. Tall trees only became popular when the Christmas tree reached the USA, and has remained a large fixture ever since.

The Renaissance and Baroque periods were marked by new influences and materials from the New World, which resulted in changing styles and a greater appreciation for flower arrangements. These arrangements were based on three techniques: filling a container with stems until full and balanced; loosely filling it with sticks and branches first, then arranging flower stems in between; or making a hole with a stick in gravel or moss and sticking the flower stem in.

Apart from these pompous arrangements, we still see the extensive use of traditional flower creations like wreaths and garlands for celebrations and parties amongst royalty and the nobility. Most common and affordable were loosely arranged flowers or a single flower put in a vase. For those with even lesser means, we see a mix of evergreens, paper flowers and ornaments.

With the introduction of Rococo from the French court, we see new fashions including table decorations consisting of a centrepiece and garlands trailing from a focal point in the fashionable C or S shapes. These shapes combined with the feminine way of using flowers epitomised Rococo design. When using winter materials, these designs take on a more rustic appearance.

Flowers at Christmas are far more recent than Christmas trees, wreaths, garlands and scattering of evergreens: the earliest flowers were introduced only 150-200 years ago. The 19th century was characterised by great changes. More effort was put into decorating homes with fresh flowers. Flowers had become easy to find on markets and in newly opened flower shops in all major cities around Europe. As the development of work and skills increased, so did the status of the profession (florist). Similarly, cultivation methods improved to such an extent that flowers were more accessible all year round.

We see the introduction of pre-cultivated flowers, manipulated to bloom in midwinter – over Christmas – like Amaryllis (Hippeastrum), Christmas rose (Helleborus), tulips (Tulipa), lilies-of-the-valley (Convallaria) and, most importantly for us, the Poinsettia (Euphorbia) during the mid to late 19th century.

The undisputed Christmas flower, native to Mexico and 3-5 meters high, was first brought to the USA in 1828 by Ambassador Joel R. Poinsett. It later spread to Europe. It is assumed that Mexican Franciscans used these flowers in the 17th century as decorations in their Christmas celebrations. However, their use goes back long before that. According

Christmas basket

Poinsettia arrangement

Hanging chandelier

to Aztec mythology, the Poinsettia got its holy red colour from a goddess who died from a broken heart. For a long time, it was used as a cut flower, because the plants are tall, lanky and weak, and thus not suitable for windowsills and tables.

Poinsettias were presented as plant arrangements in containers and baskets; often planted in waxed paper or special metal containers inside. Flowers were either mixed or only as a single variety, decorated with ribbons, dried materials, cones, nuts and fruits. Bouquets – whether inspired by nature or the Biedermeier style – came in Christmas versions too, made from evergreens, ivy (Hedera), holly (Ilex), and various dried materials and fruits, all wired and precision made. Garlands were used for both indoor and outdoor decoration. Main streets in most cities were richly decorated with garlands on facades and in between lamp posts over the streets. The wreath had changed from scaring evil off to becoming a beautifully decorated, welcoming symbol on doors. At the time, more advanced creations were popular like special Christmas baskets made from long-lasting materials, evergreens, cones, nuts and fruits which were all arranged as if they were flowers.

Poinsettia as cut flower

The late 19th century saw the introduction of vastly popular candle arrangements. These were made in many different versions like chandeliers, hanging and standing ones, wreaths and single decorated ones. These structures – made of wire, wood or both – were all dressed in evergreens like pine (Pinus), fir (Picea) or juniper (Juniperus). Even the candle holders were made from wire, circling around the basis of the candle. As they were decorated with cones, nuts and ribbons, these advanced designs were very labour intensive. A very popular version was the Advent wreath with its four candles, symbolising the four Sundays leading up to Christmas.

From the 20th century onwards, the profession continued to evolve. Proper training for florists was introduced, and exhibitions and competitions grew, thus developing the profession even more. More special flower creations were also being produced for window displays, specific events and, most importantly, Christmas. Advanced, time-consuming and technically superior creations made from scratch became common. The florist was also a carpenter as s/he created various shapes for Christmas, chandeliers, wreaths for tables and doors, and different kinds of baskets.

Techniques being used included wiring, binding and arranging. Using moss, hay, clay, wood and wires, florists' green fingers turned black from these materials. A special

19th century candle arrangement

mention should go to candle arrangements, which were made in containers or built on wooden constructions. These structures were sawn or carved into the desired shape, then painted and treated with boric acid to get a frosted snow-like surface. Later candle holders were made from wire. When made as a dry arrangement with evergreens and other materials, clay or wire was used for the arrangement. If fresh flowers were used for the arrangement, packed, watered and wired moss would be inserted.

Popular choices for Christmas were the Christmas rose (Helleborus), tulip (Tulipa), Amaryllis (Hippeastrum), Azalea, Begonia, Cyclamen, mistletoe cactus (Rhipsalis), willow (Salix), mistletoe (Viscum), hyacinth (Hyacinthus), lily-of-the-valley (Convallaria) and the Poinsettia (Euphorbia). Other flowers included the ever present rose and carnation (Dianthus). Evergreens such as pine (Pinus), fir (Picea), ivy (Hedera), and holly (Ilex) were also popular. Lots of dried materials were used, often painted in another colour or given a frosted surface. These were combined with various candles, ribbons, cones, nuts, fruits and artificial accessories like bells and miniature Santa Clauses. A lively imagination and highly creative mind was not wasted either!

Not much changed during the first half of the 20th century. The biggest change came about in the 1950s with the invention of floral foam. However, arranging styles did not

Mid 20th century candle arrangement

change much because of this: the decorative style still dominated. From the 1970s onwards designs became more diverse and gave birth to formal-linear and vegetative styles. In later years, the transparent and other more individual styles came about reflecting the personality of the creator. For a long time, man celebrated the birth of Jesus at Christmas; before that ancient peoples celebrated the winter solstice. However, the religious importance has diminished the last 150 years. Therefore, Christmas has become a secular holiday and a social event for family and friends in many countries around the world across different religions.

Because of this, we can draw on a wide range of designs and different materials to use. Christmas celebrations in Europe and the rest of the Northern hemisphere are very different from those in Asia, Australia and South America. Using influences from other parts of the world, today's marvellous choice and quality of flowers and other materials and combining these with our knowledge and inspiration from the past challenge us to develop and reinvent designs and flower use for Christmas.

Flowers have always been a part of the celebration of Christmas and have so much potential when combining traditions and new ideas. Christmas is a time of hope, happiness and rejoicing. So, flowers have to convey these emotions surrounding the festive season. Show people how flowers spread the message of joy and celebration.

Advent wreath

The future of Christmas flowers

Christmas is probably the time of year we associate most with flowers for their beauty and the traditions surrounding them. We have used flowers for their colours, scent and the messages they send to keep our traditions alive over many centuries. Depending on how you look at it, it may be a good thing or a bad thing. On the one hand, designs stayed the same for many years, showing no visible development. If this is because people only want traditional designs, florists cannot be blamed. We do see a decline in the use of flowers at Christmas. The reason is that people's homes look different today, modern. So, these homes are in need of new designs too. We think this situation opens up many opportunities for florists.

Looking back at history, we see many beautiful, skilfully created, and often time-consuming arrangements, which are all highly decorative. Yet, today we consider them traditional. For many people, cut flowers in a vase or single plants in a beautiful container epitomise modern design. We have to show arrangements and bouquets that appeal to people's current tastes, by means of updated, contemporary design.

Allow modern people to maintain their traditions but in new and expressive ways that match their stylish homes. Traditions need to be adjusted and modernised to meet the demands of life in the 21st century. We need to invent ways of dealing with our traditional flowers and materials to give them their rightful place in modern society. This can be done by coming up with more expressive designs which use new materials whilst staying true to tradition.

We are not saying you should work with new materials only, because nature – as a source of material and inspiration – is and always will be very important at Christmas. As you will see in this book, we can work with natural materials to create clean, modern and contemporary designs. Other possibilities include new accessories in a wide range of materials and colours, again inspired by tradition but with a modern touch.

Many people are looking for something new in cut flowers, bouquets and arrangements. Something personal that represents their lives and demonstrates their originality. This book can help them express themselves by means of our suggestions and creations.

We often look at traditional flowers and designs, thinking that we would like to have them in our homes, but more often than not, they just don't fit in. We want the old but with a modern twist.

Christmas is celebrated around the globe, by people of all beliefs and nationalities, with their family or friends. We must remind people that, by using technology, they can give flowers at Christmas to their loved ones wherever they may be. We must think globally in terms of design, marketing and sales. We can spread the joy of Christmas; the infinity of family ties, the giddy depths of love and the nourishing warmth of friendship. Aren't we fortunate that Christmas returns every year?

Step by step

Needle plate

Designer
Max
Materials
Pinus
Zantedeschia
Phalaenopsis 'Garnet Glow'
Anthurium andeanum
Vanda
Epidendrum
Tillandsia dyeriana
Arachnus
Bird fruit
Iron frame
Chicken wire
Spray glue
Spray paint
Spool wire
Glass tubes

Design A classic design using only Christmas materials. The pine needles create a strong yet playful look. The flowers stand in sharp contrast to the base. You can remove the flowers and replace with fresh ones, which means it can be used for the entire Christmas season.
Technique The pine needle bed is made on an iron construction covered with small chicken wire. Its strength lies in the glued needles. The wreath on the edge is composed of flowers in glass tubes, held in place by the bird fruit. The long stalks of the flowers create long, flowing lines.
Emotion The pine plate creates feelings of warmth and the smell of Christmas while the wreath reflects the colours associated with the festive season. Traditional in inspiration, modern in look.

Needle plate

1 Make an iron frame, using bars 4 mm in width. Cover the frame with chicken wire. Make sure the wire is tightly stretched and tied. Spray with fir green paint.

2 Remove needles carefully from the Pinus stem so that they are still attached in pairs. Weave them horizontally into the wire in all directions to look like dense undergrowth.

3 Spray the needles with glue and push them tightly together with both hands. Insert small glass tubes around the edge of the plate and fill with water. Attach with spool wire, if necessary.

4 Make a wreath using the bird fruit along the edge. Place the flowers in the glass tubes, using those with the longest stalks first to create a flowing line. Use the smaller ones to complete the arrangement.

Fresh and festive table wreath

Designer
Max
Materials
Tillandsia xerographica
Ludisia
Cambria
Jasminium polyanthum
Kalanchoe pumila
Reindeer moss
Christmas balls
Black glass plate
Glue pistol

Design This Christmas ball wreath can be used over and over again. A versatile base to work from: use different flowers to create many new looks. If you use small flowers, it will look natural with a lot of details.
Technique When you are preparing the base, make sure the balls and plate are clean and not too cold, otherwise the glue will not adhere. Remove all leaves to create a transparent effect; place flowers in one direction to simulate movement. Fill the balls with water.
Emotion Christmas balls glued into a wreath create an element of surprise. Fill them with fresh orchids for a luxurious feeling.

1 Remove the copper head and hooks on the Christmas balls. Glue the side and bottom of the balls to the glass plate. Make sure everything is clean and dry before you start.

2 Arrange the shiny, matt and coloured balls randomly. Fill the empty spaces with Reindeer moss, making the wreath compact.

3 Fill the Christmas balls with water. Do this very carefully as water could loosen the hot glue. Although cold glue is stronger, it is more difficult to work with.

4 Put the flowers in the Christmas balls, starting with the Jasminium which creates a pretty line, followed by the biggest flowers and those with longer stems. Place the flowers randomly.

Royal Advent

Designer
Tomas
Materials
Different orchids
Apples
Pine needles
Strong iron wire
Christmas balls (different sizes)
4 candles
Flat, round dish
Sand
Gold spray paint

Design A classic arrangement in shape and colour with a modern touch. The 4 candles symbolise the Advent period. They are the focus point of the arrangement, reinforcing the period leading up to Christmas. The gold-coloured wire supports the idea of opulence. One does not have to fill the vase with flowers and decorations, as the frame shrinks the capacity of the vase.

Technique Creating a golden, coarse texture on the frame is an innovative technique as is waxing the orchid stalks. By doing this, the flowers stay fresh longer, without using floral foam or water. This technique cannot be used for delicate flowers.

Emotion This arrangement reflects Advent. Green, red and gold are traditional Christmas colours: warm and cosy.

1 Make the collar of the arrangement from iron wire. Bend it into curly shapes of various sizes. Next make two wire circles. One has to be slightly smaller than the circumference of the dish; the second circle should be 20% smaller than the first. Connect the two circles by arranging the curly wires between them. Use tape and binding wire to attach the various pieces to one another. Spray the wire construction with glue and dust with sand to create a coarse texture.

2 Spray with gold paint. Cut the orchids off the stem and wax the tip of every stalk.

3 Fix the wire frame into the vase using hot glue. Put 4 candles in the middle; scatter the pine needles; and arrange the apples and Christmas balls randomly in the vase.

4 Attach the flowers to the frame using cold glue. Place some flowers on the pine needles. The orchids are ideal as they are resilient.

Light in the dark

Designer
Per
Materials
Ilex verticillata
Nerine
Malus fructus
Vuylstekeara Cambria
18-gauge wire
Bullion wire
Metal angel's hair
Red spray paint
Plastic water tubes
Floral tape

Design A modern version of candles and candle rings integrated into one piece. The idea is to take old traditions, update and present them in an innovative manner. It is a durable creation that uses few but expressive flowers.

Technique The wire technique again, integrated into the candle to create the impression of lightness and elegance. Structure should be placed ⅔ down from the top of the candle. Use the biggest possible plastic water tubes to ensure ample water supply.

Emotions In the cold, dark season we want warmth and light, and a cosy atmosphere where we can light candles and see flowers inside the house. Flowers, as symbols of hope and warmth, remind us of Christmas.

1 This long-lasting structure is made of Ilex berries and flowers in glass tubes. Cover the tubes with floral tape; add metal angel's hair then attach and smooth the tail-like shape with bullion wire. Wind bullion wire around the angel's hair to even it out and make it stay in position.

2 Start by piercing the wire 2 cm into the candle. Make sure that you work in a horizontal line around the candle. Heat each wire before piercing the candle. This helps to prevent damage to the candle.

3 When all wires are inserted, take a new wire and start weaving a chicken wire. Where the wires cross, twist them together twice as you work your way around the candle. (See p. 73 for exact description.) Then make a second and third loop, depending on the desired size.

4 Spray the entire structure red. Once it is dry, cover with different coloured metal angel's hair. Fasten with bullion wire, worked over and under the structure, criss-crossing each other. Attach Ilex and rose fruit to the structure. Finally, add the flowers in the tail-like water tubes.

Christmas treasure

Designer
Per
Materials
Poinsettia
Picea abies
Malus fructus
Ilex verticillata
Christmas balls
Glitter stars
Soil
18-gauge wire
Red and purple spool wire
Mizuhiki wire
Red glass container
Clear Life

1 Start by preparing all the decorative elements needed for this plant arrangement. Wire and floral tape Christmas balls to long sticks. Attach Malus apples of different sizes to tips of sticks; wire bits and pieces of Ilex using red Mizuhiki wire; and stick pins in the glitter stars.

2 We use 18-gauge wire and coloured spool wire to make the structure and then cover it with Picea (ordinary green).

3 Make an 18-gauge wire structure (see p. 73). Cross 2 wires midway. Twist them together 3 times. On the first cross, add more wires, each time crossing the existing wire in 2 places, twist together and continue to form a spider's web.

4 To make this difficult 3-dimensional widening structure, start at the bottom and work your way up. Put it in the container from time to time to adjust the direction and size of the structure. Keep the distance between wires at 5-7 cm to allow the weaving of Picea branches.

Design See the potential of plants. Poinsettia is updated to create a modern, decorated arrangement reflecting the spirit of Christmas. Use plants as you would use cut flowers, mix and work in shapes and surfaces. We need to show that plants are a part of floral design too.
Technique When working with plants always make sure that you use enough soil for that plant. This is necessary for stability and durability. Even if the structure is not perfectly formed, it will change once you attach the Picea firmly. Apply *Clear Life* to the structure to ensure that flowers stay fresh longer.
Emotions Eye candy for Christmas! A bowl filled with the promises of a rich and happy Christmas.

27

Christmas treasure

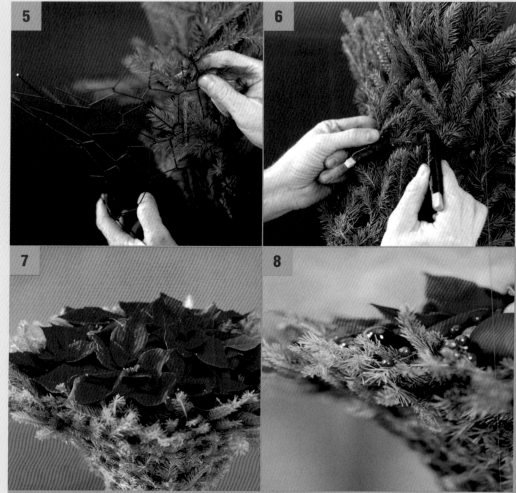

5 Use longer Picea branches – 15-25 cm in length – to exit the structure at the top. Use shorter branches further down. Weave and overlap until the wire structure is no longer visible. Consider using the lightest and finest branches at the top edge.

6 Use spool wire to flatten the outer side of the Picea covered structure. Work with different shades of red wire to tighten and secure the branches. Tie wire evenly over the whole surface and in different directions.

7 Place the finished structure in the container. Add soil for stability, plant the big Poinsettia and add more soil. Plant the Poinsettia in level with the Picea structure edge or slightly above.

8 Place all prepared decorative elements in between the Poinsettia petals, slightly grouping them to create a rich, colourful surface. Work out towards the edges with smaller, lighter materials, to emphasise the crown shape.

Wax wreath

Designer
Max
Materials
Helleborus niger 'Christmas Glory'
Wax
Pinus (needles)
Straw wreath (50 cm in diameter)
Wallpaper glue
40 glass tubes (1.2 cm in diameter,
length 8 cm)
Handmade paper

Design Various elements make this structure extra-ordinary: wax, needles coming out of the wax, and the way they are arranged. As the glass tubes are completely submerged, it seems as if the flowers are also growing from the wax base. A truly surprising design.
Technique Prepare the paper pasting a day in advance. Work very precisely, making sure that the whole wreath is covered in wax. The needles should have the same length. Remove the foliage from the Helleborus.
Emotion Pine needles, wax, Christmas roses and a wreath are classic Christmas materials. By using them in an unexpected way, we get a result that is modern and innovative. The look is clean and sober, creating a feeling of peace and quiet.

Wax wreath

1 Drill 40 holes in the wreath and insert the glass tubes. They should stick out 5 mm above the surface.

2 Make liquid glue – mix wallpaper glue powder with water – but a bit stronger than normal. Tear the handmade paper into irregular pieces (about 3 cm). Dip the pieces, one by one, into the glue and cover the wreath. Do twice (2 layers) for the best result. Leave to dry for 24 hours.

3 Melt the white wax (you also can use white candles) into a liquid and leave to cool down for a few minutes. If very hot, the wax will be too thin and transparent. Paint the wreath until the crust is very thick and textured.

4 Select long Pinus needles. Pick them carefully so that needles are still attached in pairs. Place them – about 8 mm apart – on the wreath and fix with liquid wax.

5 Fill the glass tubes with water and insert the Helleborus. The flowers are just slightly higher than the needles.

Pearls of romance

Designer
Tomas
Materials
Ranunculus asiaticus
Phalaenopsis
Wax flower
Cineraria leaves
Orchid roots
Aluminium vase
Artificial snow
Wreath of branches
Dried Musgo branches
Silver wire
Christmas balls

Design A classic arrangement with a modern feel. The opening in the middle creates a calming effect. By using an aluminium vase combined with grey branches and the soft purple, pink flowers, we achieve harmony. The colour grey has the ability to support other colours.
Technique Building a construction, fixed on a ready-made wreath demands a certain level of skill. But once you have the construction, you can use it repeatedly. The structure holds the flowers in the right place. To change the water, remove the construction from the vase and pour it out.
Emotion The classic wreath is always a popular Christmas arrangement. By merely using different colours, materials and techniques, we can change the look. In this case, the colour creates a relaxed, soft even romantic feeling.

1 Put a pre-made wreath in the aluminium container. Add dried branches to this base. The branches should spill over the edge, downwards. Tie the branches with thin, silver iron wire.

2 Use hot glue to fix Christmas balls to the branches. Divide them equally over the arrangement. Use shiny and matt balls. Vary the size of the balls (maximum 3 sizes).

3 Stick the flowers directly into the vase. (The container is already filled with water.) Start with the Ranunculus, followed by the other botanical materials e.g. wax flowers, orchids etc.

4 Add some Stachys leaves and finish with orchid roots on top. These touches will soften the static, bulky design. 35

Extravaganza

Designer
Per
Materials
Poinsettias
Malus fructus
Ilex verticillata
Soil
Red glass container
Christmas balls
Glitter stars
Mizuhiki wire

Design Christmas plant arrangement, very common in Sweden but losing popularity fast to bouquets and arrangements. As these plants are tough, they will last the entire Christmas holiday. Make them as irresistible, colourful and modern as any other arrangement and decorate them richly and they will again become popular.
Technique Plant normally, but deeper so that the flowers are close to the edge of the container; accessories are used to build upwards and outwards. Remember to leave 2 cm free between soil and edge of container, to prevent water spilling over.
Emotions Rich, colourful almost in the spirit of an American Christmas. Be bold, go for a lavish and extravagant design!

1 For this plant arrangement, we need low, sturdy mini Poinsettia plants and lots of decorative materials. More is more, in this case! Start by preparing the materials. Stick wire into the smaller Malus, and wooden sticks into the bigger ones. Stick wire into the Christmas balls and floral tape to secure them.

2 Attach a stick to the centre of a star. This will later help you to position transparent stars.

3 Plant the Poinsettia deep, so that the red petals touch the edge of the container to create a domed effect. Remove most visible foliage. Group the plants, creating empty spaces for the decorative materials.

4 Place big stars between the Poinsettias, working in layers. Finally add smaller and transparent ones to overlap with other stars. Extend the shape, working stars out over the edge to create an elegant effect. Connect and lock the materials in position using vertically wired materials.

5 Finally add apples, Christmas balls and Ilex. Work some horizontal lines of Mizuhiki wire with pierced on berries and apples over the arrangement. Interweave all material to create a decorative, mixed look.

Exotic Christmas

Designer
Max
Materials
Banana musa
Cranberries
Ilex verticillata
Vanda
Pine cones
Small pine cones
Cosmosam
Strelingea
Litchis
Rambutan
Cold glue
Glass vase
Clear Life

Design This banana flower is decorated in a cone shape, using traditional Christmas material (pine cones) combined with exotic fruit. The fruits symbolise those which ancient tribes used to celebrate the shortest day with. So do we, but in a more exotic way.
Technique Glue the cone shape with the biggest materials first; fill in the smaller fruits later. Use the press-remove-press technique when gluing heavy objects. Remove one petal from the banana every day to help it stay beautiful for longer.
Emotion We create a bright, happy feeling. Place the bananas in a group like a family. It will create a relaxed atmosphere.

1 Fill the bottom of a vase with cranberries; place the stem of the banana on top of the berries. Fill with water and top up with cranberries. By repeating the red, the composition becomes balanced.

2 Prepare the fruit material. Cut the pine cones in half (in the length) and then slice finely. Clean all the fruit with a dry towel to remove all water.

3 Glue the fruit to the banana. Squirt some glue on the fruit and leave to dry for 15 seconds; press against the banana, and slowly pull it off again, creating glue wires. Repeat a few times until they have bonded.

4 Look at the shape of the banana and start to glue the biggest fruits in between and follow the shape. On the end fill the open spaces with the smaller fruits and slices of the pine cones. Spray Vanda flowers with *Clear Life*. Glue them to the cone, thus reflecting the brightness of the banana flower.

Pine cone nest

Designer
Per
Materials
Pinus fructus
Pinus
Skimmia japonica
Hypericum
Ranunculus
Panicum
Rosa fructus
Cymbidium
18-gauge wire
Spool wire
Floral tape
Plastic tubes with stem

Design Another decorative bouquet – my all time favourite item! Working with natural materials gives an almost rustic feel, but with a very distinct and modern look. This bouquet is voluminous but uses few flowers. Cones are decorative and take the place of foliage.
Technique Radial tied bouquet made with structures from pine cones. The most important aspect is the stability of the pine cone layers. This can be done by locking pine cones tightly into one another, using pliers. This is the only way to create a flat, slightly domed profile.
Emotions The element of nature will always be very important at Christmas. The smell of pines and pine cones is strongly associated with the holiday season too. This bouquet marries tradition with modern style in a striking manner.

1 Long-lasting materials in various shades of brown starting from the pine cones and blending into red, grey-green, orange and a little yellow.

2 Materials needed: spool and stub wires, plastic water tubes with a stem. Use open, round pine cones, that can easily be interlocked, as this is crucial for the design. The surface of this structure should be dense, flat and slightly domed.

3 Place the Cymbidium flowers in the plastic water tubes. Stems should be as long as possible. The water supply should last long enough.

4 The structure is made using only cones and wire. Start by wedging 2 or 3 cones into one another and tie them tightly together with wire. Use pliers, if needed. Add more cones to the first, in the same way. Tie everything together, until you reach the desired shape and size.

41

Pine cone nest

5 I made 2 crescent moon shapes for the bouquet design. Tie all spool wires very tightly together. Then make the handles. Take 3 stub wires, fold them double and insert from the top into the cone structure. Tie to the spool wires and twist all the wires together using pliers. Cover with floral tape.

6 Bend all handles in towards the centre of the bouquet. To stabilise and create the circle, use short pine branches. Cut and clean the branches below the spiral. Then cut the exact length for the diameter of the bouquet.

7 Insert flowers in between the pine branches, in a spiral pattern; and all flower heads following the domed profile. Start with sturdy flowers and insert fragile ones, such as Ranunculus and Cymbidiums, last.

8 Finish the bouquet by adding pine branches to the base for sheer beauty and strength. Tie together with a spool wire in a matching colour.

Proud Amaryllis

Designer
Per
Materials
Hippeastrum
Pinus
Pinus fructus
Rosa fructus
Dianthus
Skimmia japonica
Cymbidium
Berzelia lanuginose
Spool wire

Design This design shows off the Amaryllis in all its splendour. The pine cone structure creates a smaller and refined basis which balances the heavy flower, without competing for attention.
Technique Parallel bouquet with a structure. The pine cone layer provides aesthetic appeal as well as stability to the top heavy Amaryllis. When making the structure, work with a precise and firm hand. Make sure the holes for other plants and materials are exactly the right size. Add material both above and under the cones to ensure balance.
Emotions Amaryllis has become the flower most associated with Christmas, even beating the Poinsettia to it. Warm, proud, generous and long lasting, it makes the perfect gift during the Christmas season.

1 Remove foliage from flowers and some of the pine needles on the stems on the longer pine branches. Avoid a heavy, messy look. Elegance is the word!

2 The structure – with a hole in the middle – is made by interlocking pine cones and tying them together with spool wire. Wedge 3 cones tightly into one another. Tie tightly together: wire should touch the stem of cones. Twist wire ends together with pliers. Make more sets in the same way and attach to other sets. Make sure that the spool wire is not visible.

3 Position the pine cone layer two-thirds down from the Amaryllis flower. The hole in the layer must be the exact size of the stem, not smaller. The irregular empty spaces will be used for the other flowers – to stabilise the Amaryllis.

4 Add flowers and other material both under and over the pine cone layer to stabilise it. Work most flower heads all the way down, level with the pine cones. But, be careful not to cover the pine cone structure. Arrange all stems parallel and tie together with spool wire in a matching colour.

45

United we stand

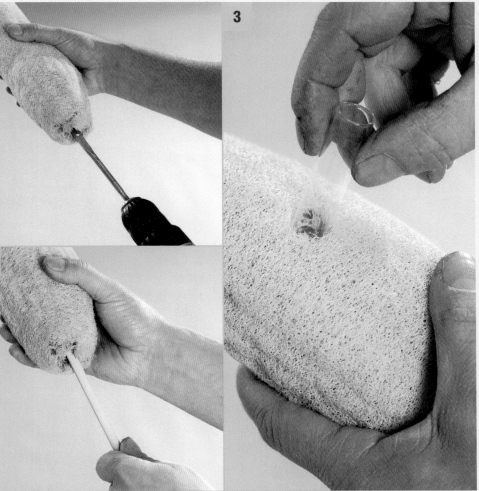

Designer
Max
Materials
Cryptomeria
Pine needles
Phalaenopsis
Paphiopedilum
Hypericum Green Condor
Chrysanthemum Rocky
Cold glue
Mizuhiki wire
9 long, green loofahs
Iron bar (6 mm) on a square base
Glass test tubes (1.2 mm wide, 8 cm long)

Design The intention is to create a fresh arrangement with lots of detail: robust yet fine. Traditional Christmas greens are combined with bright, fresh green. The separate loofahs are united to form one family, living in harmony.

Technique After making the base, stick Cryptomeria and pine needles direct into the loofahs. Make a robust, transparent field (7 cm thick). We add intensity and colour with Japanese mizuhiki wire; the Phalaenopsis, Chrysanthemum and Hypericum add a lot of detail. Finally, the Paphiopedilum in the glass tubes, creates interesting lines. The last layer of pine needles adds the final touch to the arrangement.

Emotion A symbol of personalities connected in a subtle way. It shows the symbioses between different characters, highlighting the strong personality of each in a positive and playful way.

1 Take 9 long loofahs with different shapes. Drill a hole (6 mm wide and 10 cm deep) into the bottom of every loofah. Drill straight, as the angle of the hole will determine the direction in which the loofah will turn.

2 Weld an iron bar (6 mm wide, 20 cm long) to a square base. Paint it the same colour as the loofah. Apply cold glue to the tip of the bar and push into the hole. Make sure the loofah and its base are stable.

3 Drill 1-2 holes (12 mm diameter, 8 cm deep) into the side of the loofah. Make sure the holes in the loofahs are at the same height. Drill at an angle to prevent water from running out of tubes. Insert glass tubes.

United we stand

4 Place all the loofahs at an equal distance from one another. Make sure the glass tubes point inwards.

5 Join the loofahs horizontally using Cryptomeria. Stick them into the loofah, as they can last long without water. Do the same with the long pine needles, 7 cm in depth.

6 Cut the Mizuhiki wire into pieces. Stick wire into a Hypericum berry or a Chrysanthemum and then into the loofah, filling out the layers between the loofahs. Insert the orchids into the tubes. Prepare some Phalaenopsis with *Clear Life* and glue some in between the other material. Finish the arrangement with an extra layer of pine needles, so that everything is connected and forms a field of flowers.

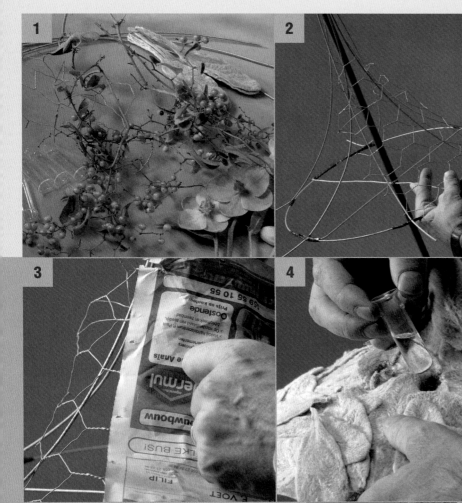

Velvet softness

Designer
Tomas
Materials
Helleborus
Stachys byzantina
Smilax berries
Strong iron wire
Chicken wire
Spray glue
Glass tubes
Cetraria islandica
Newspaper

Design A Christmas tree is always a sure-fire winner. The classic Christmas tree has been given a new look. The shape is important as it gives the tree a modern twist. Little space between the vase and the tree is important as it creates balance and proportion. Using only one kind of flower and branch makes this a creation that captures the essence of Christmas.

Technique The sky is the limit. Beauty lies in the shape of the structure and not the type of material. Bind and model the iron to make any shape you wish. Use thicker wire for the base and finish with smaller ones. This tree can be used for many years as the materials lend themselves to recycling.

Emotion Simplicity shows the beauty and pureness of a single material. The soft, velvet leaf structure of Stachys reminds us of something gentle and calming.

1 An arrangement built on an iron structure. Working with Helleborus requires using glass tubes which hold water. The shape of the vase is very important as it determines the shape and design of the arrangement.

2 First make a metal structure. Start by making a circle. The circumference has to be bigger than that of the glass container. Place two wires inside the circle to form a cross. Attach these to the circle. Place a stick upright where the wires cross and fix to the construction. The length of the stick will determine the height of the final structure. Add more upright wires to create a flowing tree shape and fasten the top ends to the central stick.

3 Cover the structure with chicken wire; it will consolidate the whole surface. Spray the structure with glue and stick on newspapers. Glue overlapping Stachys leaves to newspaper, using cold glue. Start at the top and work your way down. Glue some leaves to the edge; and natural Icelandic moss to the bottom.

4 We use typical Christmas flowers, Helleborus, for this design. This delicate flower has to be put in water immediately. For this reason, we use glass tubes. Push the tubes into the structure.

5 Finally, add some Smilax branches. Insert the flowers into the water-filled glass tubes.

51

Firey horns

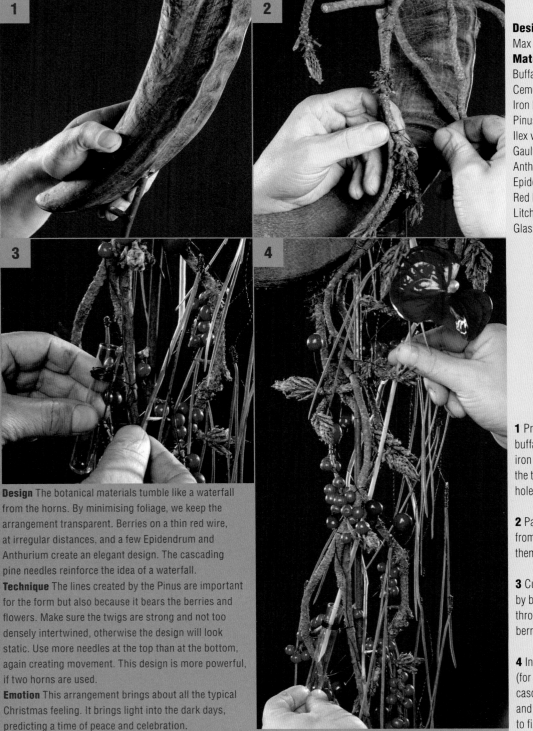

Designer
Max

Materials
Buffalo horns
Cement
Iron bar (6 mm wide, 50 cm long)
Pinus
Ilex verticillata
Gaultheria berries
Anthurium andreanum
Epidendrum
Red bullion wire
Litchis
Glass tubes

Design The botanical materials tumble like a waterfall from the horns. By minimising foliage, we keep the arrangement transparent. Berries on a thin red wire, at irregular distances, and a few Epidendrum and Anthurium create an elegant design. The cascading pine needles reinforce the idea of a waterfall.

Technique The lines created by the Pinus are important for the form but also because it bears the berries and flowers. Make sure the twigs are strong and not too densely intertwined, otherwise the design will look static. Use more needles at the top than at the bottom, again creating movement. This design is more powerful, if two horns are used.

Emotion This arrangement brings about all the typical Christmas feeling. It brings light into the dark days, predicting a time of peace and celebration.

1 Prepare all the material. Drill a hole of 6 mm into the buffalo horns. Fill an empty tin with cement; position an iron bar in the centre; and leave to harden. Once dry, cut the tin away. Stick the other end of the iron bar into the hole (of the horn) and fix with glue.

2 Paint the iron bar and base black. Remove all needles from the Pinus. Drape the twigs over the horns. Bind them with red bullion wire.

3 Cut the Ilex verticillata into small pieces. Make a chain by binding pieces to the red wire; weave these chains through the Pinus. Do the same with the Gaultheria berries. Place 9 glass tubes in each structure.

4 Insert the flowers, starting with the Epidendrum (for long lines); then the Anthuriums; and, finally, cascading pine needles. Use bullion wire for the flowers and glue for the needles. Spray needles with glue to fix them.

53

Scarlet red

Designer
Tomas
Materials
Cambria red
Rosehip
Natural Musgo moss and branches
Artificial snow
Cold glue
Hot glue
Dry floral foam
Large, upright vase
Skewers

Design The shape vase and the tree are eye-catching as they mirror each other's shape. Vases can inspire us to use extraordinary shapes and designs in a modern arrangement. When colour meets design, they become one.

Technique Sculpting your own base provides many new possibilities and challenges. Dried floral foam is the ideal material to use. In this design, two kinds of glue were used: hot and cold. Hot glue can be used with non-living materials, such as Musgo branches, mosses, etc. Use cold glue for fresh material as it will not burn botanical material.

Emotion The spirit of Christmas ... translated into harmony. The red colour and the tree shape flowing into each other reflect the intensity of the moment. Let the intensity of colour and shape enchant you.

1 The V-shape of the vase mirrors the shape of the tree. Cambria orchids can be glued to moss as they can last long without water.

2 Cut the dry floral foam into a tree shape. Mould it until you are satisfied with its form. To smooth the surface, file with a piece of dry floral foam.

3 Glue Musgo branches to the floral foam. Glue moss randomly to follow the tree shape, using hot glue.

4 Glue the berries with cold glue to the moss. Use cold glue, otherwise they will burn and turn brown. To create movement and tension, arrange them to spiral from the top to the bottom.

5 Glue the Cambria flowers to the tree, using cold glue. Glue the stalks before attaching them to the moss. They will stay fresh longer.

Hidden treasure

Designer
Tomas
Materials
Vanda
Musgo branches
Cinneraria
Transparent glass Christmas balls
(3 different sizes)
Artificial snow
Hot glue
Candle wax
Styrofoam ball
Spray glue
Cotton wool
Floral foam wreath

Design In this arrangement, the focus is drawn to the inside of the vase. By using bulky and rough surfaces combined with delicate flowers, we highlight the fragile beauty inside. The artificial snow gives it an all winter look.
Technique Working with cotton wool and artificial snow we create a snow landscape. Spray glue is the best to use with this technique. It is better to glue Christmas balls directly onto the plastic surface of the floral foam wreath because of their weight when filled with water.
Emotion Truly beauty lies inside; the only treasure worth searching for is your own nature.

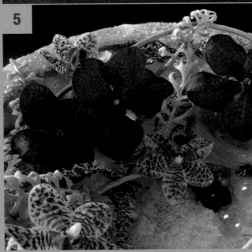

1 The idea is to have an arrangement within a spherical vase, which needs to be big, round and rimmed. Cut a slice from a Styrofoam ball and place in the vase. Spray paint the Styrofoam grey to match the colour of the vase. The paint will burn into the Styrofoam, resulting in a rocky structure. Dribble with hot candle wax.

2 Place the foam wreath in the vase. Glue transparent balls to the bottom of the plastic plate but not the foam. Their openings should face up. Put cotton wool between the balls to cover the floral foam and the inside of the vase.

3 Spray the arrangement with artificial snow. For colour, add a few small purple Christmas balls. Add some Musgo branches. The arrangement should look appealing and inviting. Tie some branches randomly to other materials to ensure the natural flow of growth as your inspiration.

4 Wind purple iron wire around the stems of the leaves to make them look even more decorative. This will also consolidate the design.

5 Stick the orchids into the glass balls and fill with water. Do not cover the whole arrangement with flowers as the snow landscape has to be visible.

57

Christmas arch

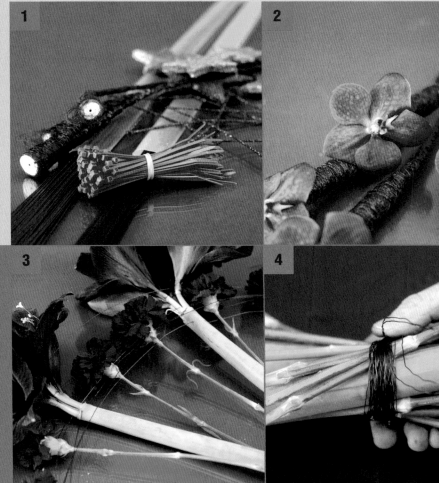

Designer
Per
Materials
Hippeastrum
Rosa 'Passion'
Alstroemeria
Chrysanthemum
Ilex verticillata
Dianthus
Vanda
Mizuhiki wire
Spool wire
Plastic water tubes
Metal angel's hair
Floral tape
Glitter stars
Plastic cable ties

1 Remove foliage from all the flowers. We want to create a clean look that focuses on the flower arch and not the stems. Use Mizuhiki wire for the structure and lots of stars to decorate. Wire the tubes with 3 pieces of 20-gauge wire, floral tape them and cover in metal angel's hair. Tie everything with bullion wire.

2 Fill the tubes with water and insert the orchids – their stems should be as long as possible. Use a cap that really closes tightly around the stem. These 'tails' have a technical use too: they stabilise the structure, once inserted between the stems.

3 Make an arch using carnations and Amaryllis. Remember to thin out the arch towards the ends by placing bigger flowers closer to the centre. Pierce the carnations in the lower, sturdier part of the flower head and the Amaryllis in the stem. Work in an overlapping and crossing manner to create stability and take strain off single flowers.

4 Once all flowers are connected and others in place – all in a spiral formation – tie them with spool wire in a matching colour; make a thick decorative binding point. While doing this, keep the bouquet on the table as not to break any stems.

5 Increase the volume sideways by using bigger transparent stars and orchid tails. Use pins and cable ties as needed. Finally, decorate with more stars and cut Ilex branches, gradually thinning out the arch towards the ends.

Design The structure of the bouquet allows us to add other flowers – with their own water supply – in different ways, lots of accessories and materials, which dry beautifully. So, the final result is a cross between a bouquet and an arrangement.
Technique Bouquet, radial in the shape of an arch. Be careful when piercing the flowers and do not lift the bouquet up until you have tied the stems together. Ensuring stability below and at the top (flower level) is the most important aspect.
Emotions Elegant, light and transparent with lots of materials and details. Christmas designs need to be freed from their heavy and rustic history! Present flowers in the way people relate to.

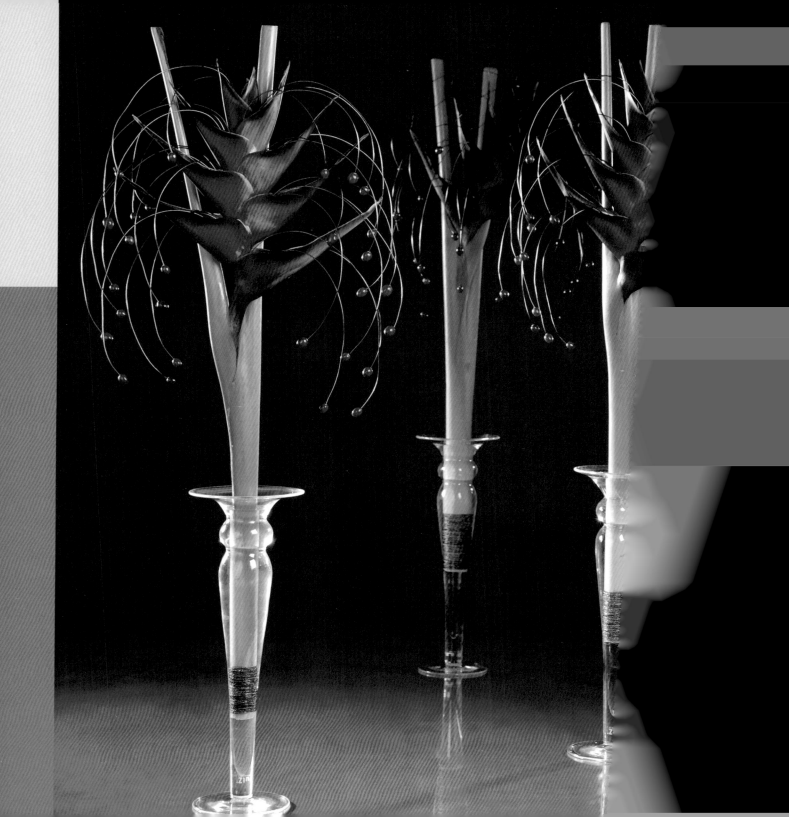

Heliconia fountain

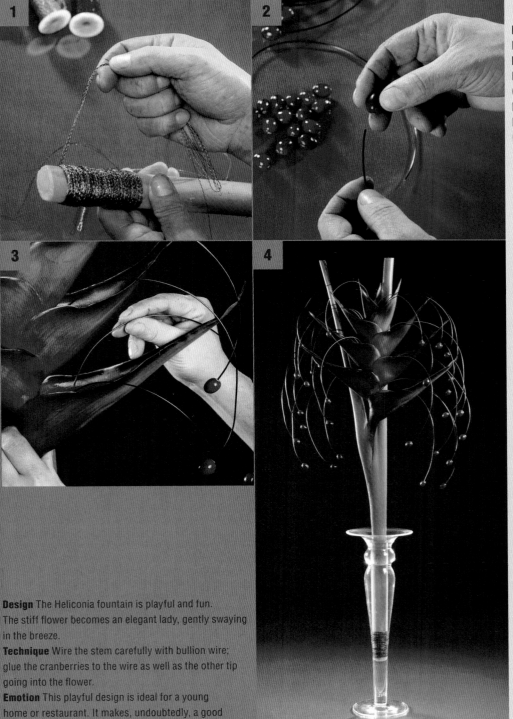

Designer
Max

Materials
Heliconia stricta
Cranberries
Red and pink bullion wire
Red aluminium wire
Cold glue

1 Wind red and pink bullion wire around the stem of a red Heliconia, covering about 12 cm.

2 Cut red aluminium wire into different pieces of 20 to 25 cm. You will need 30 per flower. Stick a cranberry into the tip and fix with cold glue.

3 Slice the end of the wire diagonally. Stick this sharp tip into the Heliconia flower. Start at the bottom, using the longest wire. Work upwards, each time using a shorter wire to create a fountain effect.

4 Put the Heliconia in a glass vase and fill it with water. The bullion wire looks much bigger in the water bigger. It also creates a good colour balance with the flower. A group of these will make a strong statement in any setting.

Design The Heliconia fountain is playful and fun. The stiff flower becomes an elegant lady, gently swaying in the breeze.
Technique Wire the stem carefully with bullion wire; glue the cranberries to the wire as well as the other tip going into the flower.
Emotion This playful design is ideal for a young home or restaurant. It makes, undoubtedly, a good conversation topic.

61

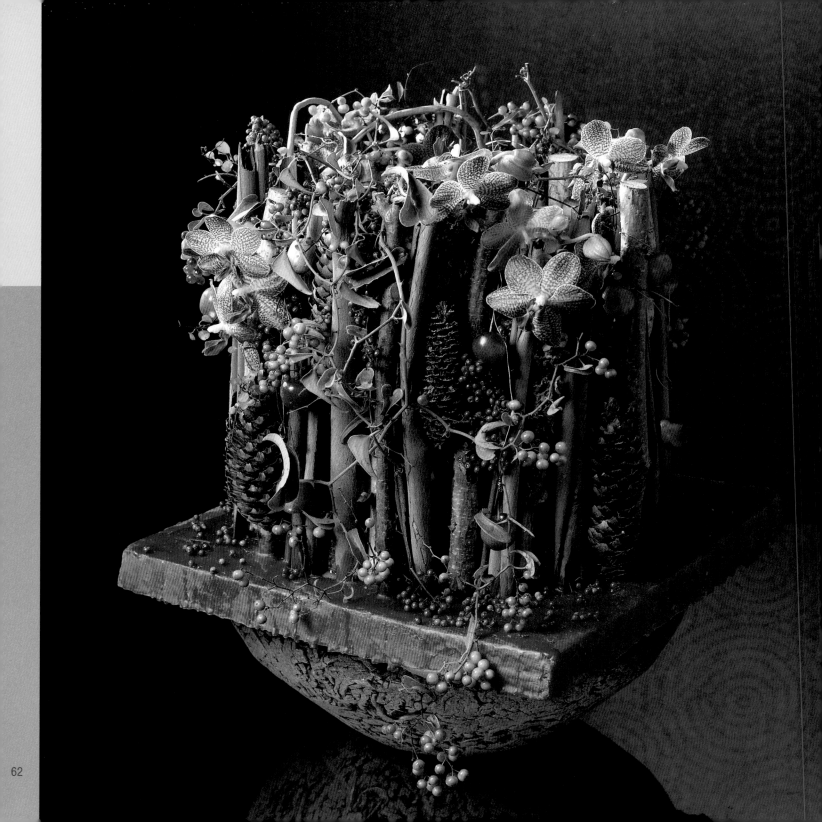

A scent of beauty

Designer
Tomas

Materials
Phalaenopsis
Phalaenopsis roots
Red dried peppers
Malus
Pine cones
Eucalyptus bark
Betula
Plastic tubes
Mushroom moss
Perfumed red candles
Floral foam (red)

Design Placing a square shape on a round container is not an obvious choice as it challenges our vision. Perfumed Christmas candles add to the splendour of the design. Although the branches are very close, they do not touch each other. So, there is a sense of transparency and lightness.

Technique Several techniques are used for this arrangement. Firstly, 'painting' with perfumed candle wax, and using an existing shape and red floral foam. The opening of the vase is very small. So, placing the big square of floral foam on it gives us the freedom to make the arrangement as big as we want to.

Emotion When smelling the perfumed candle wax, we immediately think of Christmas, the joy and celebrations it brings.

1 The basic materials of this arrangement are important. The coloured, square floral foam plate makes it possible to work with branches. The use of perfumed candle wax will give this arrangement an extra dimension.

2 Draw a circle in the floral foam to outline the shape. Stick the branches into the foam. Use Betula and Eucalyptus branches.

3 'Paint' the surface with wax to give it a more decorative appearance. Use perfumed wax that smells of Christmas. Drip some extra wax around the branches, as it will make the construction sturdier.

4 The pine cones add to the Christmas feeling. Glue them to the branches at different heights. Cover plastic tubes with brown mushroom moss.

A scent of beauty

5 Glue the plastic tubes, pine cones and dried red peppers to the branches. Place them on the inside and outside of the branches.

6 Insert flowers into the water-filled, plastic tubes. Weave the Smilax through the branches. Wire the apples and stick into the wood. Place the orchid roots.

Pine needles

Designer
Per
Materials
Pinus japonica
Ranunculus
Nerine
Skimmia japonica
Ilex verticillata
Glass tubes
Floral tape
Floral Fix
Rubber band
Bullion wire

1 Different shades of red in flowers and berries. Red is the colour of Christmas! Harmony is more important than contrast at Christmas.

2 Make a basis by taping glass water tubes to each other. Take one, apply 2 layers of *Floral Fix*. Arrange 6 tubes around it and press lightly together. Finish by taping 2 layers of floral tape around the tubes.

3 Insert long pine needles (bunches of 1 cm each) in the openings around the tubes. The *Floral Fix* will stop them from sliding out. Make sure all ends are levelled.

4 Use a rubber band to keep the pine needles in place. Make a wide decorative binding point with a mix of different red and purple bullion wires. Their colours will complement the red layer of flowers and berries at the top.

5 Fill the tubes with water, and insert a mix of flowers at the same height as the tips of the pine needles. The whole structure should grow outwards. Finish by sticking single Ilex berries to some pine needles, to create movement.

Design Playing with material and finding new uses and looks in tune with tradition. The idea came from an upturned broomstick: appealing in its simplicity with its perfect lines and distances for arranging flowers!
Technique Arrangement in glass tube structure. Stability and size of glass tubes are crucial here. Level the tubes and the pine needles at the bottom for good stability. Use bigger glass tubes to avoid constant refilling of water; also use flowers that need less water.
Emotions A new look for Christmas! Long pine needles with their darker ends at the bottom, getting lighter upwards and giving way to flowers that open and create a warm, red feeling. Playful with traditional materials.

Growing moss balls

Designer
Max

Materials
Straw
Plastic bucket
Iron wire (1.2 mm wide)
Spool wire
Tape
Cornus alba siberica
Gaultheria procumbens
Moss
Wooden sticks

1 Tape wooden sticks lengthwise to a plastic bucket. The sticks should extend 15 cm on both ends of the bucket. Use 6-7 sticks per bucket. Do not use wire but rather tape as it keeps the sticks firmly in position.

2 Tie spool wire to a stick, winding it around the bucket. Place thin layers of straw between the wire. Weave the wire between the wooden sticks. Continue padding the ball with straw until you have reached the size you need. Make sure the ball is sturdy and robust before you continue with the next steps.

3 Take pieces of iron wire to attach moss to the straw ball. Use clean, fresh moss. Start at the top and work your way down to the bottom.

4 Fill the ball with soil and plant the Gaultheria procumbens. Cover the soil with moss.

5 Cut the Cornus into smaller pieces, about 10 cm in length. Wire 1 piece to form 2 'legs'. Stick these legs into the moss, draping them over one side of the ball and the Gaultheria plant.

Design This moss ball – made from natural material and filled with plants – will last longer than fresh flowers. Use it as an outdoor decoration too. Many variations on the theme are possible with this design.
Technique Make sure the Cornus sticks are firmly attached to the wire, as it will ensure that the shape remains in place. This cascade of sticks creates movement and harmonises the various materials.
Emotion The combination of materials and a round shape create the idea of a huge Christmas decoration, bringing with it feelings of peace and harmony.

Blooming pine spheres

Designer
Per
Materials
Pinus fructus
Ilex verticillata
Malus fructus
Poinsettias
Christmas balls
Floral foam balls
18-gauge wire
Mizuhiki wire
Soil

Design Recreated pine cones. A modern basket, made from traditional Christmas materials, showcasing a traditional flower, the Poinsettia. By re-inventing our traditional materials, we give these flowers a well-deserved place in a modern home.

Technique Planted and decorated arrangement in dry foam. The crucial aspect is to cut deeper in the middle as to avoid water to spill over. The pine cones sphere asks for precision work: bigger and smaller cones have to fit properly. It is important to make the bottom slightly flatter than the rest to ensure stability.

Emotions Natural and traditional in material and structure, yet modern in look. Allowing modern people to connect with traditions but in a new, expressive way that matches their stylish homes. Traditions need to be adjusted and modernised according to the current trends.

1 Plant arrangement in a container made from pine cones to give it a botanical look. Use round, open pine cones. You have to be able to wedge them into each other to give the sphere a flat surface.

2 Wire the pine cones individually. Bind a wire mid-way around the cone and twist tightly together. Use pliers to help you. It is important that wires are firm as they give the sphere stability.

3 Start cutting out a slice of the sphere. Cut deeper in the centre. Insert cones from the bottom, working your way to the top. Remember to wedge the cones into each other. This will put them in position.

4 When you get to the top, use different sizes to create an interesting line. Fill the cavity with as much soil as possible. You do not need plastic, as the dry foam is waterproof. Add the accessories on the sides and over the Poinsettias to extend the line.

Christmas stars

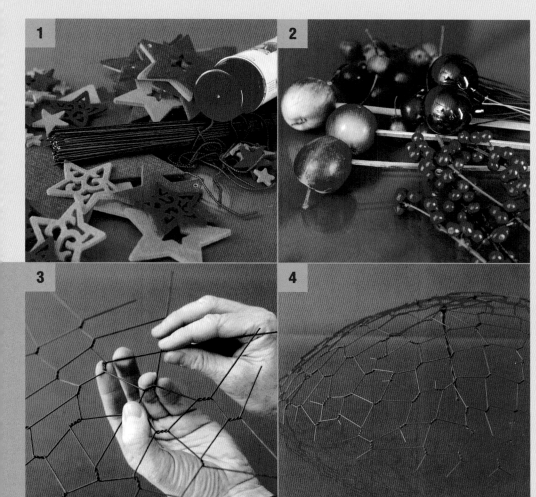

Designer
Per
Materials
Ilex verticillata
Gloriosa rothschildiana
Malus fructus
Poinsettia
Rosa 'Passion'
18-gauge wire
Bullion wire
Christmas balls
Glue and glue gun
Red spray paint

Design The classic decorative bouquet is made of a structure that allows us to use fewer materials, have a stronger non-green colour look and draws the eye to the Poinsettia and Christmas star. The focus is on flowers and their colour and not the foliage.
Technique Radial tied bouquet in a structure. Making the structure is difficult, but the end product is worth it. Do not use chicken wire to simulate the structure, as it will not give you the same domed effect. You *have* to make it yourself.
Emotions The bouquet radiates warm, generous, cheerful, joyful Christmas emotions symbolised by the stars. Poinsettia and felt stars make a bouquet suited to the modern person who appreciates old traditions meeting new trends.

1 For this bouquet, we use lots of felt stars glued on to an 18-gauge wire structure. Other materials such as paper and cardboard and shapes can also be used in the same way.

2 Prepare all decorative materials, sticks and wires in the apples; wire the Christmas balls and Ilex branches, securing with floral tape. Remove all foliage from flowers when only flowers heads are used in the final bouquet.

3 Make 18-gauge wire structure. Cross 2 wires midway. Twist them together 3 times. Add more wires, each time crossing the existing wire in 2 places, twist together and continue to form a spider's web. Keep the distances between the wires smaller in the centre, to allow them to expand towards the edges. This will ensure stability. Continue to add new wires until you reach the desired size and shape.

4 When finished, make a handle. Attach 3 wires, each in a different place to the structure. It should form a triangle in the centre. Fold them inwards, connect their ends and twist them together. Finish by covering the wire with floral tape. Spray paint both sides red. This will help the structure to blend in better with the final design.

73

Christmas stars

5 To apply the felt stars, use a mix of glue and weaving technique to get a sturdy structure. Start with a few bigger ones, weave the ends into the structure, then glue them from the bottom. Continue connecting other stars on the upper side, using the bigger ones as the base, constantly overlapping.

6 Blend colour and shapes in a harmonic pattern, working your way out over the border of the wire structure. Make sure you end with lighter and more transparent stars for an elegant touch. Leave an opening in the centre and some space between the stars for the flowers and accessories.

7 Start in the centre with heavier flowers and fruit – like roses and apples –, work outwards using lighter, fragile flowers – like Poinsettia and Gloriosa. Remember to place the stems in a spiral system, to prevent them from breaking. Work in an overlapping manner. Finish by gluing transparent stars on top of the flowers to connect all parts.

Christmas flow

Designer
Tomas
Materials
Different orchids
Orchid roots
Acrylic
Nylon thread
Christmas balls
Glass tubes

Design This design is ideal as a Christmas table arrangement. The materials would complement a modern interior. The transparent acrylic gives it a light and soft feeling. The unusual Christmas balls in different colours add to the festive feeling. An uncluttered, playful design.

Technique The most difficult part is to thread all the material. Do not force the acrylic or put too much pressure on one fish line: divide over various lines, otherwise they will snap. New materials make new techniques possible. Use transparent nylon thread as often as possible.

Emotion By using transparent acrylic together with many, brightly coloured Christmas balls, we can create a dreamlike, light and floating emotion. The honest and clear design reflects the same emotion. Less is more.

Christmas flow

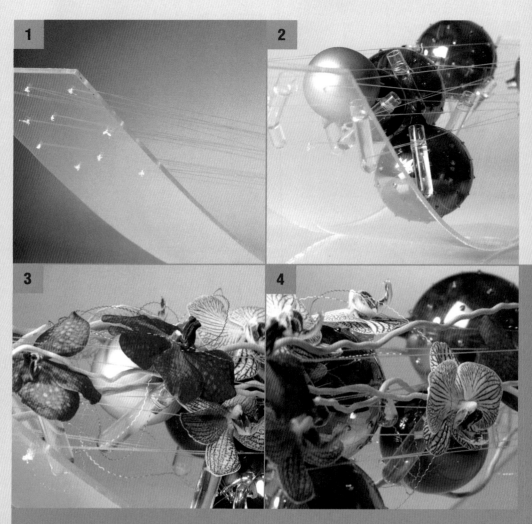

1 Take a piece of acrylic 16 x 100 cm. Drill a few holes into both ends and bend into a concave shape. Ease the nylon thread through the holes and tie the ends together.

2 Suspend the Christmas balls between the lines and then do the same with the glass tubes. Make sure the tubes are upright and securely placed. Use nylon thread to fasten them to the other threads.

3 Place more balls and flowers on the left than on the right to create tension in the design. Put various kinds of orchids in the glass tubes.

4 Finish by arranging some orchids roots on top to add horizontal lines to the design. Thread some coloured wire through the arrangement to make it even more festive.

Parallel Christmas

Designer
Per

Materials
Hippeastrum
Ilex verticillata
Nerine
Dianthus
Chrysanthemum
Alstroemeria
Phormium
Steel grass
Rosa 'Passion'
Tulipa
Malus fructus
Red glass container
Coloured floral foam
Glitter stars
Pins

Design Parallel modern arrangement with plenty of variety, characters and lines! When mixing many materials, make sure you show the life and character of all the materials. By removing all foliage, you reinforce the idea of movement of these proud flowers.

Technique Arrangement technique in coloured foam without covering it. Plan where you put the stems as there is no second chance. Cut the foam to fit into the container, 1 cm below the edge. Remember to use the height of the volume and the lines to criss-cross so that they can create movement.

Emotions A strict, clean, modern look but full of movement and life. Restrained at first, but upon close inspection, a generous and welcoming arrangement.

1 Remove all foliage from flowers. Lines and transparency are crucial here. We will arrange a lot of material in a small container to highlight volume, depth and height. Stick Hypericum berries onto Steel grass and put pins in the glitter stars.

2 Create lines by placing coloured sticks first; then add the Amaryllis. Place the sturdiest ones first and then thinner more flexible stems into the volume, moving from side to side. Remember to work from top to bottom, and inside and out, thus adding to the volume.

3 Finish with the steel grass: secure them within the other stems by weaving them around the stems. Insert wired and pinned accessories, grouping them throughout the arrangement. Remember to create rhythm and volume. You do not want to have a flat surface!

4 Finish by attaching glitter stars to the tops of coloured sticks, thus covering the ugly ends and balancing the cylindrical volume. They also serve to mirror the bottom, emphasising the cylinder shape.

Towering grace

Designer
Tomas

Materials
Anemone
Jasmine
Kochia leaf
Populus alba branches
Christmas balls
Hot glue
Glass tubes

Design Transparency of the construction, the use of 5 dishes and the decorative and functional aspect of the Christmas balls make this eye-catching arrangement a joy to look at. Towering grace in all her glory.

Technique Making a construction is not always easy. Start by placing the sticks on the dishes, to stabilise the bunches. Tie the branches in at least two places to ensure stability. When fixing the Christmas balls, remember to glue them in various places to different branches.

Emotion This arrangement gives me a sense of a community. Five different identities complement each other. That's what Christmas is about: infinite family ties, deep love and the nourishing warmth of friendship.

1 Arrange 5 triangular dishes pointing towards each other. Tie the branches together. The bunches are denser at the top than at the bottom. This ensures stability and supports the aesthetic.

2 Fix Christmas balls – the hole facing up – to the branches with hot glue. Note that the balls will be filled with water, so make sure they are glued in several places.

3 When all balls and glass tubes are fixed, fill the Christmas balls with water and insert the foliage. There is no need to tie the foliage, just squeeze them between the branches.

4 Guide the jasmine through the branches. This is not only decorative but also functional: they will hold the flowers in place. Divide and place the different flowers randomly. Make sure there is a balance in colours because the purple anemone is rather dominant in the arrangement.

Delicate balance

Designer
Tomas
Materials
Orchids
Meuhlenbeckia
Orchid roots
Tillandsia xerographica
Populus alba
Boll moss
Iron base
Strong iron wire
Chicken wire
Hot glue
Shiny black sticks
Christmas balls
Spray glue
Newspaper

Design The strength of this arrangement lies in its shape. To make the container look more powerful, lessen the dominance of flowers. Using the Christmas balls as mini vases adds to the Christmas spirit. The flowers can be changed regularly without any difficulty. The container is the main feature and can easily be used as a table arrangement.
Technique This technique of modelling strong wires enables us to create any shape. We don't have to use ready-made containers. Make sure that the base construction – the 2 bars in this example – is strong enough the carry the weight of the arrangement.
Emotion The flowers and materials are well balanced in the overall arrangement. Is this not what we should strive for in life?

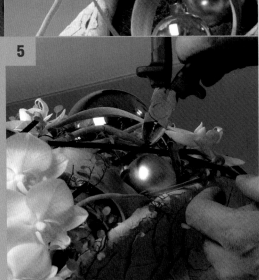

1 An iron frame on which we build our arrangement. Take 2 iron bars and bend them slightly to form a bridge. Place one bar over the other. Use strong iron wire to shape the form. Cover the bars with chicken wire.

2 Spray structure with glue and cover with newspaper. Fix the Populus alba leaves to the newspaper, using cold glue (to avoid burning the leaves).

3 Fill up the middle part with boll moss and glue the balls to each other or the inner wall. As they will be used as water containers, their openings should face upwards.

4 Start adding the botanical elements. Take the Tillandsia and spread them randomly across the length of the structure. Next, insert the Phalaenopsis and Meuhlenbeckia into the glass balls. Arrange some orchid roots between the flowers to break the monotony of the strong, straight lines.

5 Add some shiny black sticks to refine the shape. Do this by tying them to and weaving through other materials.

Stars

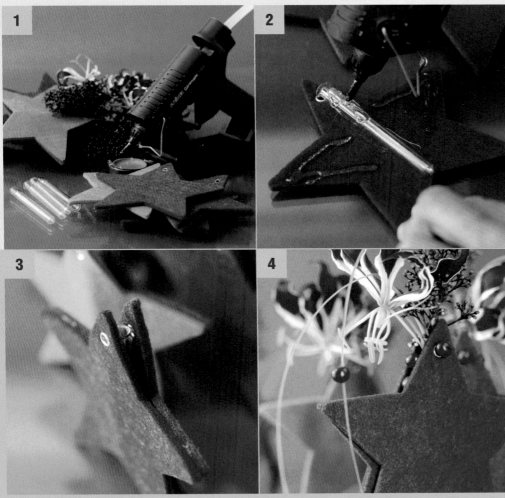

Designer
Per
Materials
Ilex verticillata
Skimmia japonica
Gloriosa rothschildiana
Xerophyllum tenax
Felt stars
Glass tubes
Glue and glue gun

Design Using the symbolism of the Christmas star results in a modern, almost childish creation. Individual and strong design with a few traditional flowers. Use many to create a mass arrangement.

Technique Vase arrangement consisting of flowers in various glass tubes. Glue 2 stars together. Then fix the stars, part the lower 'legs' and stabilise them. You can insert single or casually mixed flowers in the different tubes. Adjust the size of the glass tubes to the watering needs of the flowers. Make sure the stems go all the way down.

Emotions These walking Christmas stars have a child-like feeling of hope and expectation, associated with Christmas. Something joyful, but still with the symbolism of Christmas. Place a row of stars to serve as a table decoration. Single stars can be given as gifts!

1 Stars made of felt or any other sturdy material; paper or cardboard to make a stable container. Clean foliage from all flowers. Stick Ilex berries on the Bear grass. Pierce berries with 19-gauge wire to make a hole.

2 Attach the glass tube to one star, using hot glue. Use enough glue to attach 2 stars to the side and top of the tube. Press together and hold for 1-2 minutes.

3 Do not glue the 2 lower pointy ends together. This helps to stabilise them. Separate and bend these 2 'legs' outwards.

4 Glue single Ilex berries between the stars to cover the tube. Fill with water and put the newly cut flowers in. The stems should be covered in as much water as possible.

Oh oh apple tree

Designer
Max
Materials
Black spool wire
Apple tree branches
Apple tree twigs
Acrylic
Broken green glass
Foam for dried flowers
Glass vases
Cold glue

1 Unroll 1 spool wire and scramble it until you have a loose mass of wire resembling a tree shape. Take a thick apple tree branch and firmly insert into the wire mass.

2 Cut a bit of the stem (on the side) away to form a flat surface. Take another stem and do the same. Tie the stems together, flat surfaces facing each other, in 2 places.

3 Now you cut the small ends of the apple tree in small pieces about 5 centimetres long and tie them in long spool wire into long chains. Don't make the distance in between the wooden pieces too long (3 cm), prepare 15 of 1,5 meter long of them.

4 Fill the centre of the wire tree with twigs. Once that is done, wind the strings around the tree until it reaches the desired shape and size.

5 Push the tree into the foam, pressing the 2 stems together. Once in, they will split open and remain like that. Cover the foam with broken glass. Cut thick green-yellow acrylic in little squares and cold glue them to the tree.

Design It is a modern variation on the pine tree: vibrant colours and shiny materials make everything about this tree a jolly spectacle. The perfect alternative to the traditional pine tree; ideal for small rooms.
Technique Make sure the wire structure is not too tight. Take great care when tying the two stems together, as their stability is vital to the design.
Emotion Young and modern in execution, classic in form. The bright colours bring a smile to your face, reflecting the joy of the Christmas season.

Honoured Christmas rose

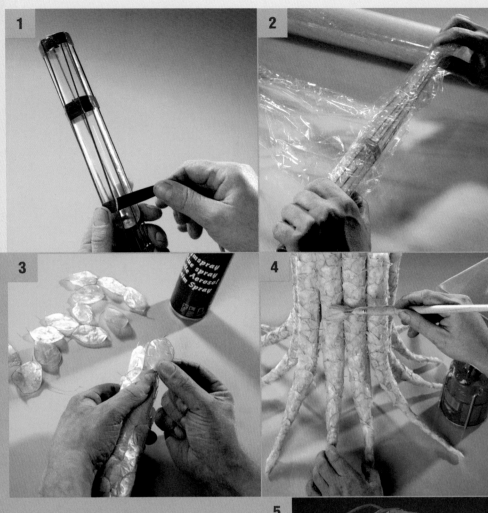

Designer
Max
Materials
Large glass tubes
Lunaria
Wax
Iron wire (1.5 mm wide)
Tape
Orchid roots
Helleborus niger 'Christmas Glory'
Spray glue
Cold glue

1 Arrange 9 wires around a glass tube and tape them securely to the tube. Use long wire to ensure that about 10 cm of wire extends beyond the end of the tube. This part will later form the base. Make 15 pieces.

2 Roll the pieces in cling film until the surface is smooth. Bend the extended wire end of the piece slightly outwards. Repeat for all the pieces. The curve of all the pieces should look alike.

3 Spray the bleached Lunaria fruit with glue and attach to the stem. Start from the top and work towards the base. Place the leaves as to create a layered structure. A new layer starts in the middle of the preceding leaf to create overlap.

4 Using cold glue, attach all the stems to form a cylinder. Insert glass tubes without stems. These tubes will add stability and hold the flowers. Paint the stems with warm liquid wax to create a textured surface. When the wax is too hot, it will become too transparent.

5 Bend orchid roots into a round shape and place it on top of the Lunaria, spilling over the edge. Insert the flowers into the glass tubes.

Design This elegant decorative object is made to focus on the Helleborus. By using the minimum material, we draw the eye to its beauty and strength.
Technique Take great care when making the base as its shape is essential to the design. Make sure the wax is not too hot, otherwise you will not get a grainy texture.
Emotion This elegant, classical design breathes peace and purity. Yet, the beauty of the Helleborus belies its strength and power.

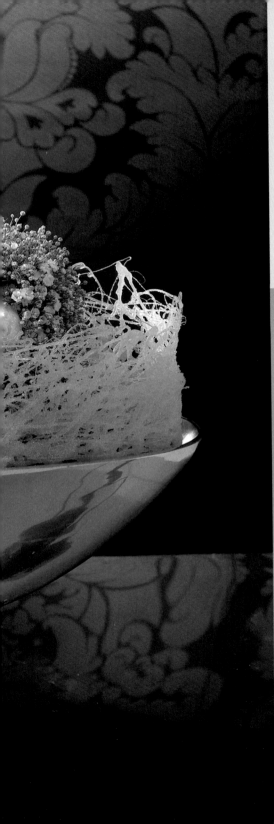

Icing on the cake

Designer
Tomas
Materials
Gypsophila
Christmas balls
Hot glue
Floral foam
Wooden skewers
Moss ball
Artificial snow

Design The centre of the arrangement looks strong, bulky and male. By crowning it with iced lace, we add softness and femininity. The design is balanced.
Technique This arrangement contains two interesting techniques. The first is to cluster material to be able to add them easily; the second is the use of hot glue as a decoration. By using flowers – such as Gypsophila – that dry well, this arrangement will last the entire Christmas season.
Emotion The rough feeling of the centre, contrasting with the delicate outside, evokes emotions of harmony and equilibrium.

Icing on the cake

1 Cut floral foam into a rectangular shape. If you use small foam bricks, join them with wooden sticks. Cut the top of the floral foam to have the right shape as this will make it easier when you stick the flowers in. Use pin holders to fix the floral foam in the container.

2 Immerse the floral foam in water, remove the sticks and put back into the vase. Fill the openings with boll moss. Put a stick in the opening of a Christmas ball and fix it with hot glue. Arrange the balls randomly on the foam base. Spread the different sizes evenly over the foam.

3 As it is almost impossible to put the Gypsophila flower by flower in the floral foam, rather cluster them. It is best to prepare many clusters before sticking them in.

4 This is the most difficult part of the arrangement. Stick Gypsophila clusters one by one into the foam. Follow the rectangular shape of the floral foam.

5 Give the arrangement a special twist by making a 'net' of hot glue. Squirt hot glue onto a wet surface. The design should resemble a net. Make the lower part of this glue net thicker and stronger than the decorative upper part. The lower part will provide stability.

6 Spray with fine artificial snow to give it a frosted look. Place the net on the arrangement. Glue the two ends together. Your masterpiece is ready!

Future, creations & step-by-step instructions
Per Benjamin (SE)
Max van de Sluis (NL)
Tomas De Bruyne (BE)

History
Per Benjamin (SE)

Drawings
Kathy Kim (Korea)

Photography
Kurt Dekeyzer (BE)
Helén Pe (SE)
Pim van der Maden (NL)

Proofreading
Ilze Raath

Final editing
Mieke Dumon (BE)

Layout & photogravure
Graphic Group Van Damme, Oostkamp (BE)

Printed by
Graphic Group Van Damme, Oostkamp (BE)

Published by
Stichting Kunstboek bvba
Legeweg 165
B-8020 Oostkamp
Belgium
tel. +32 50 46 19 10
fax +32 50 46 19 18
info@stichtingkunstboek.com
www.stichtingkunstboek.com

ISBN-10 90-5856-207-7
ISBN-13 978-90-5856-207-4
D/2006/6407/35
NUR 421

Per started working with flowers at an early age and
started his consultancy company Benjamins Botaniska
in Stockholm. He has won over ten medals in national
and international competitions. World champion in 2002
and Scandinavian champion in 2003, he now teaches,
exhibits and demonstrates all over the world.
per@life3.net

Max, born and bred in the Netherlands, owns a flower
shop in Zeeland. He works for companies worldwide,
finished third place in the 2002 World cup and got the
second place in the Europe cup. Max gives seminars and
demonstrations all over the world.
max@life3.net

Tomas, Belgian floral designer, has his own flower shop
in Wenduine. He became fifth on the world cup in 2002
and won at the same time the 'Quality and Freshness
Award' for the best technical work. Tomas gives seminars,
demonstrations and realises decorations all over the world.
tomas@life3.net

Life3 – emotions, creativity, craftsmanship and communi-
cation. This co-operation, the first of its kind between
three florists, is working to add new value to the flower
industry, take floral design to new levels and bring it
to a wider audience. This international co-operation
offers demonstrations, workshops, decorations, shows,
seminars, books, education, trend information and
more within the world of flowers and beyond.

a bundle of creativity www.life3.net